Goofy Government Grants & Wacky Waste

Sheryl Lindsell-Roberts
Illustrated by Myron Miller

Sterling Publishing Co., Inc.
New York

Library of Congress Cataloging in Publication Data

Lindsell-Roberts, Sheryl.
    Goofy government grants & wacky waste / by Sheryl Lindsell-Roberts : illustrated by Myron Miller.
       p. cm.
    Includes index.
    ISBN 0-8069-3858-7
    1. Waste in government spending–United States–Anecdotes. 2. Government spending policy–United States–Ancecdotes. 3. Federal aid to research–United States–Anecdotes.
I. Miller, Myron, 1948– II. Title.
HJ7537.L56 1996
336.3'9'0973–dc20   96–21075
                                                           CIP

10 9 8 7 6 5 4 3 2 1

Published by Sterling Publishing Company, Inc.
387 Park Avenue South, New York, N.Y. 10016
© 1996 by Sheryl Lindsell-Roberts
Distributed in Canada by Sterling Publishing
% Canadian Manda Group, One Atlantic Avenue, Suite 105
Toronto, Ontario, Canada M6K 3E7
Distributed in Great Britain and Europe by Cassell PLC
Wellington House, 125 Strand, London WC2R 0BB, England
Distributed in Australia by Capricorn Link (Australia) Pty Ltd.
P.O. Box 6651, Baulkham Hills, Business Centre, NSW 2153, Australia
Manufactured in the United States of America
All rights reserved

Sterling ISBN 0-8069-3858-7

Dedicated to my husband, Jon
(who was the inspiration for this book and for so many
wonderful things in my life!)

Alphabetical Acknowledgments

A special thanks to . . .

Marc Abrahams, publisher of *Annals of Improbable Research* (the Journal of Record for Inflated Research and Personalities). If you'd like to learn of ongoing government waste, you can subscribe to AIR, Box 380853, Cambridge, MA 02238. A one-year subscription to this wonderful journal is available in the United States for $19.95, $27 in Canada, and $40 overseas. Or you can receive an electronic newsletter containing the tidbits that were too small for AIR by sending Marc an e-mail message at marca@wilson.harvard.edu.

Kris LeFleur, my research assistant. At the time of this writing Kris was an aspiring young writer studying at Boston University. Kris, I hope to see your name on the best-seller list one day, along with mine.

Peter J. Sepp, Director of Media Relations, National Taxpayers Union, for sending me "Outrage! Of the Month," published in *Capital IDEAS*. This publication is issued ten times a year. If interested, contact National Taxpayers Union Foundation, 325 Pennsylvania Avenue, SE, Washington, DC 20003.

Leslee Sherrill-Spoor, Press Representative for Capital Cities/ABC, Inc. Leslee was kind enough to send me transcripts of Sam Donaldson's ABC *Prime Time Live* interviews on Washington waste.

CONTENTS

A Funny Thing Happened 7

Preamble 9

1. Traveling Travesties 11

2. Critter Capers 25

3. Crazy Country Costs 35

4. Absurd Armed Forces 47

5. Food and Fun 59

6. It's All in the Delivery 65

7. Citizen Beware 72

8. Mixed Messages 81

Wacky Wasters Hall of Fame 91

About the Author 93

Index 94

A Funny Thing Happened on the Way to the Post Office...

I scurried off to the post office to mail two envelopes. One was this manuscript, which I was sending to my editor, Sheila. The other was my estimated quarterly taxes, which I was sending to my uncle, Sam.

As I approached the counter, I overheard two postal workers talking about a government study that had been done to determine how many calories we ingest when we lick a stamp. "Calories ingested licking a stamp?" I questioned. "Yeah," one of them replied, "I don't know how many calories we actually swallow, but can you believe that stamps have calories? And that the government spent our money on this wacko study?"

I scratched my head, wrinkled my brow, and thought about the contents of the manuscript I was about to mail. Add whatever that postal study cost to:

- $19 million to explore gas emissions from cow flatulence
- $800,000 to install a restroom at the top of Mt. McKinley
- $2 million to construct an ancient Hawaiian canoe
- $500,000 to build a replica of the Great Pyramid of Egypt in the State of Indiana
- $1.8 million to prepare a topographical map of two parishes in Louisiana
- $145,000 on a wave-making machine for a swimming pool in Salt Lake City
- $150,000 to study the feud between the Hatfields and the McCoys . . .

With all this wacky waste, does the government really need this check I'm about to mail? But who am I to question the wisdom of our Washington wizards.

Quest for Knowledge

So, as a writer with an insatiable appetite for knowledge, I decided to find out more about where our tax dollars are going. I don't know the outcome of all these studies. Some may still be in progress. Some of the results haven't been made public. Some may have had funding withdrawn after the absurdities were made public. In any event, I've uncovered some lulus. You really have to wonder—with all the ills of this country (poverty, drugs, crime, etc.)—why money is being spent on these projects. As you read this book, you may, like me, begin to question everything from the stork to the law of gravity. And perhaps that's a good thing . . .

SHERYL LINDSELL-ROBERTS
MARLBOROUGH, MASSACHUSETTS
MARCH 1996

Preamble

Once upon a time, in Greek mythology, there was a gent named Jason. Jason sailed forth with fifty helpers in the good ship *Argo* to capture the Golden Fleece. But Jason found the Golden Fleece wasn't a pushover. Among other obstacles, it was guarded day and night by a never-sleeping dragon. Do we, as taxpayers, have a never-sleeping dragon to see that we don't get fleeced?

Senator William Proxmire, of Wisconsin, was one. He reared his head in 1975 by initiating the Golden Fleece Award of the Month for an "absurd or ridiculous or wasteful or a low priority" project. Many projects you'll read about in this book were recipients of the Golden Fleece Award. Many others could have been.

"The envelope please . . ."

1. Traveling Travesties

King of the Road

Keep On Trucking

Do over-sized trucks block your vision on the highway? Go uphill slowly? Contribute to traffic congestion? Make a big splash on wet roads? The Federal Highway Administration spent $222,000 to find out the astonishing answer: You bet they do! *(We could have told them that for a fraction of the price.)*

What Foresight!

The Federal Highway Administration proposed a bill so that truck drivers who are blind in one eye and have poor vision in the other could get driver's licenses. Fortunately, a judge had the fore"sight" to see the perils of this bill and shot it down.

Taken for a Ride . . .

The National Highway Traffic Safety Administration spent over $120,000 to test a back-wheel-steering motorcycle. Not surprisingly, it was impossible to steer.

Beep! Beep!

The National Science Foundation spent $46,000 to find out if distractions, such as sex, would decrease the honking of frustrated drivers stuck in traffic jams in cities. As bait, the agency hired bikini-clad women to roam the city streets. Instead of honking at these half-naked women, the men whistled and made lewd comments. Who would have expected . . .

The Lap of Luxury

Housing and Urban Development Secretary Samuel R. Pierce, Jr., won a Golden Fleece Award for having the most expensive limousine of any cabinet member. He was one of 190 federal officials who received chauffeur services to their homes. This cost more than $3.4 million a year.

How Many Congresspeople Does It Take to Change a Light Bulb?

"All of them," according to Judd Rose of ABC News. At least, that was the case in Chambersburg, Pennsylvania. In 1991 Congress passed transportation legislation that dictated when traffic light bulbs could be changed. For example, in Chambersburg, bulbs could be changed between 8:00 and 8:30 AM or 2:45 and 3:45 PM.

And that was one of hundreds of such projects governed by the law. It was also ordered that Chattahoochee, Florida, would get a bridge over Mosquito Creek. In New York, the Hellgate Viaduct would get a paint job. What's wrong with this, you may ask?

There was no need to put a bridge over Mosquito Creek and the Hellgate Viaduct didn't need painting.

The Ream Riddle

Q. How many pages does it take the Bureau of Land Management to request bids for fire equipment to be placed on two pickup trucks?

A. 125 pages of requirements and 23 foldout diagrams.

Runaway Spending

Fort Worth Regional Office of Urban Mass Transportation Administration (UMTA) received a Golden Fleece Award for this waste of money:

Two grants to help build bus garages to repair 150 and 200 buses, respectively. The problem with that was the fleets consisted of only 45 and 94 buses, respectively.

$1 million to replace trolley buses. The ridership at the time this was approved averaged fewer than two passengers per trip.

A Road Paved with Good Intentions

The Federal Highway Administration spent $21 million to pay for unused and unneeded roads and bridges. This is how it went:

- $900,000 for a four-lane bridge that had no road leading to or from it.

- 6.5 miles of new roadway, because traffic was supposed to double in 20 years. Somebody goofed because traffic declined by 50%.
- $26,000 for two extra-long overpass bridges because it was expected that the road underneath would be widened to four lanes. Twenty-five years after the money was invested, the road underneath remained two lanes.

Fasten Your Seat Belts

The government owns a fleet of more than 333,333 non-tactical vehicles *(and that's not counting postal vehicles)*. If you add the price of the purchase of the cars, the chauffeurs and the overhead, we're spending about $150 million each year on our cruising congressionals.

Riding the Rails

The End of the Line

The General Services Administration spent $1.5 million with a potential $13 million more–to renovate an old train station in Nashville, Tennessee, that a flock of roosting pigeons had made their home. The cleanup cost $500,000.

Who Said There's No Free Ride?

Taxpayers are spending almost $100 million each year to pay for the free subway rides of federal employees. In 1991 this bill was enacted by a Maryland Senator and passed into law by President George Bush.

And speaking of free rides. More than $7 million is spent each year by politicians on junkets to popular vacation spots around the world. It's called "business travel." As a matter of fact, when the government's fiscal year is about to run out, there's an estimated 48% increase in government business travel.

Cookoo Choo-Choo

A recent issue of *USA Today* reported what is considered by some to be the biggest boondoggle in park history. Over a period of ten years, Rep. Joseph M. McDade tapped taxpayers for $66 million to bail out rundown tourist attractions that went bankrupt after they have been moved from Vermont. *(Why they were moved from Vermont in the first place wasn't mentioned.)* One such boondoggle is the Steamtown National Historic Site Museum opened in Scranton, Pennsylvania. It's "not a monument to any critical event or location in railroad history, but a monument to the ability of Rep. Joseph M. McDade to play parochial politics," the newspaper reported.

IT'S A BIRD ... IT'S A PLANE

The Friendliest Skies

If you wanted to take your family on a year-end vacation to Puerto Rico—that's if you can afford the vacation in the first place—wouldn't you try to find the airline that offers the best deal? But, if you're a cabinet official, there's no need to bother. The Special Airlift Mission (SAM) of the 89th Military Airlift Command will fly members of Congress first class, and for free. All they have to do is call a few days in advance and a flight crew from Andrews Air force Base will be assembled. The crew will order special cuts of beef and liquors. The cost? Over $8 million a year.

Spruce-Up Time

The U.S. Forest Service won the Golden Fleece Award for "Helistat," an experimental contraption under development in New Jersey. Four helicopters were yoked to a blimp for the purpose of lifting logs from remote corners of national forests. Dubbed "the mechanical mongrel" because it was riddled with cost overruns, construction foul-ups, and inadequate planning, "Helistat" cost $40 million.

Space-y Art

Anti-object artist Le Ann Wilchusky boarded a small aircraft armed with a large bundle of crepe-paper streamers. The plane took off, and at the appropriate moment, Ms. Wilchusky threw the streamers out into the sky. She later told reporters:

"I'm sculpting in space. A black streamer looks like a crack in the sky. Red and yellow streamers look like high lines, lashing the earth. By making people look upward, my work called attention to the higher spirit of mankind."

For this "higher spirit," $6,025 was provided in a grant from the National Endowment for the Arts.

A Flying Leap

The Federal Aviation Administration (FAA) was the recipient of the Tenth-Anniversary Golden Fleece Award. The FAA received $48 million to enable municipal airports in Florida to use surplus federal land and buildings to help pay off their operating costs. At 23 of these airports, more than 9,000 acres are sitting idle because they're home to mosquitoes and sawgrass. The land has an estimated rental value of about $32 million per year. *(Where are all the realtors and developers when you need them?)*

Clip Their Wings

The Department of Defense (DOD) spent $28,000 to shuttle nine members of Congress to Washington in a posh executive jet so they wouldn't miss a close vote on the MX missile. DOD lost the vote anyway—199 to 197—so the trip was not only illegal, but a waste of time. However, to demonstrate its gratitude to these congressional cruisers, the Department flew four of them back at a cost of $16,016. The same trip on a commercial airline would have cost $1,367.

Fly-by-Night Scheme

The National Oceanic and Atmospheric Administration established the Office of Aircraft Operations (OAO) to improve aircraft management. OAO bought two helicopters for $1.9 million to be used to improve safety in the Arctic by exploring the Arctic Continental Shelf. The choppers are stationed in Miami.

From the Top Down

The Federal Aviation Administration spent $57,800 on a head-to-foot physical study of 432 female flight attendants, involving 79 specific measurements. Such measurements included the popliteal length of the buttocks and the knee-to-knee breadth while sitting.

PUERTO RICO OR BUST...

This is the saga of several families the Federal Aviation Administration (FAA) sent to Puerto Rico—with its pristine sands, hugely expensive hotels, and lavish golf courses—with our tax dollars.

The Feeney Family

The FAA transferred traffic controller Brian Feeney, along with his wife and six children, to work in the San Juan radar center. The family was housed at the ESJ Towers Hotel, overlooking the Caribbean. They stayed at the hotel for 90 days, which cost $32,400. In addition to that, the bill for their food for the first month alone was $12,419, even though their unit had complete kitchen facilities. When all the costs were added up, $77,000 was spent to feed and lodge the Feeney family for three months.

When Mrs. Feeney was questioned about these exorbitant expenses, she explained that the family ate out every night and spent about $200 for an average evening's meal. The guidelines set by the FAA allow $335 a day for food.

The Hutchins Family

Daniel Hutchins, his wife, and two very young daughters were transferred to the same center in San Juan. Their 90-day bill for food was $11,260.34. The family often ate lunch at the Taco Maker, whose basic product is a 99-cent burrito. The restaurant owner estimated that an average meal for a family of four *(and mind you, the two daughters were aged three and one)* would cost about $15.48. Why did the FAA reimburse the family $130.15 per lunch at the Taco Maker?

MORE TRANSPORTATION TEMPESTS

Motivation by Disney

The Urban Mass Transit Administration sent its officials to Disneyworld, in Orlando, Florida, to learn Disney's secrets of motivating employees. They discovered a new way to collect fares on "Space Mountain," an indoor roller-coaster-like ride. This junket cost $68,160.

Beam Me Aboard, Scotty

What will the transportation needs of earthlings be in the year 2025? Well, the Department of Transportation spent $225,000 to answer this serious question. Some of the specifications include transportation needs should the United States be:

- transformed by an Ice Age
- taken over by a dictator
- dominated by a hippie culture.

2. Critter Capers

BEASTLY EXPERIENCES

Stewed to the Gills

The National Institute on Alcohol Abuse and Alcoholism sponsored a project on aggressive behavior in fish after drinking alcohol. According to Dr. Harman Peeke, medical psychology professor at the University of California at San Francisco, fish were the only ethically acceptable subjects. It cost $102,000 to discover if sunfish that drink tequila are more aggressive than sunfish that drink gin.

Rats!

The National Institute on Alcohol Abuse and Alcoholism has also spent millions of dollars on experiments that turn rats into lushes.

And the Fish and Wildlife Service designated 77,000 acres in Riverside County, California, as a "rat preserve."

No More Monkey Business

Have you ever wondered why monkeys and rats clench their teeth? Well, the Office of Naval Research, the National Science Foundation, and the National Aeronautics and Space Administration found the answer. For $500,000 we now know that when monkeys and rats feel cheated, they get angry, scream, kick, and clench their jaws.

Does Census Make Sense?

The Comprehensive Employment and Training Act hired 101 people to go door-to-door to survey the number of dogs, cats, and horses in Ventura County, Virginia.

The Bear Facts

The Department of the Interior was responsible for passing the Endangered Species Act. As a result, a Montana rancher, named John Shuler, was stiffly fined for shooting a bear that attacked him on his own land.

This is the story: Grizzly bears had been mauling Mr. Shuler's sheep for months. One night he heard a disturbance; he grabbed his gun and ran outside. He saw four grizzlies. Three were attacking his sheep and one was running toward him. Mr. Shuler shot the bear and ran back to his home for safety. The judge fined Mr. Shuler $4,000, declaring him at fault because "he purposefully placed himself in the zone of imminent danger."

How Much Wood Could a Woodchuck Chuck If a Woodchuck Could Chuck Wood?

Once the experts at Harvard Medical School were able to repeat this tongue twister 100 times without making a mistake, they set out to get the answer. Twelve adult male woodchucks were volunteered for a two-week experiment. The experimenters defined "chuck" as 80% mastication and ingestion, 15% throwing wood around, and 5% vomiting.

Each "guest" was housed in a cage and deprived of all nourishment for one week. At the end of the seven days, each was fed through a pair of 5.08cm by 10.16cm holes in the sides of each cage. The animals were videotaped to see if they tried to:

1. eat the 2 x 4 that was offered
2. throw the 2 x 4 around the cage
3. throw up.

The findings were that all the hungry devils tried to eat the 2 x 4. *(It is likely that most of the woodchucks, however, would have thrown the 2 x 4s at the observers, if given the chance.)*

ANIMAL FITNESS

Livin' High on the Hog

How should a pregnant pig be treated? And would she be less bored if she jogged? The U.S. Department of Agriculture (USDA) studied sows that were cooped up during pregnancy, and all kinds of problems surfaced. The pigs suffered from lack of exercise and tension. So, the USDA devised treadmills for them to reduce the psychological stress on these mothers-to-be.

Stuffed Penguins

In 1994 scientists from the U.S. teamed up with scientists from New Zealand to find out why penguins in Antarctica are gaining weight. Every morning for three months the team would weigh 300 penguins immediately after they'd been fed. After the penguins regurgitated their food for their young, they'd be weighed again. *(Do you think Jenny Craig would approve?)*

Wiggling Worms

The government funded a study at the University of Washington to monitor the defecation of worms. The scientists observed one-millimeter-long worms and a mutant strain they created. Both strains were constipated.

Barking Up the Wrong Tree

The Department of the Interior spent $100,000 to train beagles to detect brown tree snakes in Hawaii. What's wrong with that? Tree snakes don't live in Hawaii; they're in Guam.

Grab the Bull by the Horns

"Bullfights and Ideology of the Nation in Spain" was the subject of a study done by the National Science Foundation to examine the dialectical relationship between the categories known as nations and regions in Spain, as they are manifested through the controversial spectacles known as bullfights. This bum steer cost $9,992.00!

Will Those Cockroaches Really Eat Anything?

The National Science Foundation gave $28,400 to a zoology professor to study the diet of desert cockroaches near Palm Springs, California.

Holy Cow!

The Environmental Protection Agency is giving Utah State University $500,000 to find out if belching cows contribute enough methane to affect global warming. The cows will be adorned with a special gizmo that will measure the volume of gas they release when they burp.

We've already paid for studies to determine the effect of cow emissions—gas at the other end—on global warming.

THE BIRDS AND THE BEES (AND THE FLIES?)

This Will Ruffle Your Feathers

The National Science Foundation is spending $155,358 for a three-year study to see if male blackbirds show off their wings to woo female blackbirds. Apparently, these "Romeo" birds spread and vibrate their feathers, and the researchers are not sure if this will get them something to chirp about.

Pigeon Economics

This relates to pigeons, but the study must have been authorized by cuckoos, because the government spent $144,000 to determine whether or not pigeons follow human economic laws.

A New Meaning to Bird Watching

The National Science Foundation and the National Institute of Mental Health sponsored a $107,000 study to understand the sexual behavior of the Japanese quail.

Project Expectations

The project was expected to "obtain evidence relevant to three sexual learning phenomena:

- sexual looking
- classic conditioning of sexual arousal
- improvement of copulatory performance with practice."

Project Results

- When a sexually mature male was placed with a female, copulation occurred rapidly, often in less than five minutes.
- Practice made perfect, as it did improve sexual performance.
- Male quail spent a lot of time staring at female quail by peering through a small window in a nearby cage.
- The "peeking" became such an event that the amorous males didn't care whether the objects of their desires were dead or alive.

Ouch! That Stings!

Now this is a honey of a deal. Beekeepers can get an interest-free government loan of 54 cents per pound of honey collateral. After the season, they have to repay only 49 cents. That's a 5-cent profit on the loan, no matter how good or bad a crop. This program costs over $100 million a year.

A Fly in the Ointment

The National Science Foundation has given $229,460 to scientists to study the sexual habits of 2,000 houseflies per week. The experiments will include creating transsexual male flies while blinding others and allowing them to mate through smell. The objective of this study isn't clear, but Gary Blomquist, the scientist heading the project, said: "We're looking at basic science here. I wouldn't even put a number on the years we need to study this. We're not even looking at control."

Protecting Smokey

An employee at the U.S. Forest Service receives an annual salary in excess of $42,000 to oversee the trademark the government holds on Smokey the Bear.

3. Crazy Country Costs

FOREIGN FRITTERS

Where Does Charity Begin?

The Treasury Department has granted a $1.2 million tax loophole to U.S. citizens who live and work in foreign countries. This loophole allows them to exclude $70,000 of their income from their income tax. Proponents argue that this tax break is needed in order to reduce the trade deficit. They allege that Americans need tax incentives in order to work overseas and sell American-made products.

Lust for Knowledge

The National Institute of Mental Health (NIMH) granted Dr. Pierre van den Berghe, a full professor in the department of sociology and anthropology at the University of Washington in Seattle, $97,000 for prostitutes. Although it's not quite what you might think, ponder this.

The money was spent to study ethnic and class relationships among Indians and non-Indians in communities in the Andean village of San Tuti, Peru—a site outside of Cuzco. The study group? Prostitutes in Peruvian brothels. Prostitutes and madams were formally interviewed over the course of eighteen months. This was part of a larger study that focused on the nonsexual *(believe that!)* functions of the bordello as a male gathering place for drinking and storytelling and as an attraction for gringos.

To add insult to injury, the good professor submitted a brief report to NIMH and wrote a book on the subject. Even though the book was funded with tax dollars, he refused to give the agency a copy.

The Grand Pooh-Bah

Moroccan visitors, staying at the Watergate Hotel in Washington, ran up a tab of long-distance telephone charges totaling $499.68. The Moroccan Embassy told the Department of Defense (DOD) that if it wanted to collect, they'd have to go to Morocco. So—in its infinite wisdom—DOD did! As taxpayers, we ended up spending $32,264.41 to recoup that $499.68.

DOD also spent $15,532.50 for a Colombian dignitary to visit Florida and then Washington, DC. This funding included the rental of a yacht to have lunch on. The main menu—filet de taxpayer.

We're Not Alone

If you think the United States has a monopoly on waste, think again! The government of Japan funded a seven-year study to determine whether earthquakes are caused by catfish wiggling their tails.

FEDERAL FOLLIES

The Paper Palace

Each year, since the National Archives was set up in 1934, it adds to its collection what equals a football field–360 × 160 feet (108 × 48m)–of paper, piled 37 feet (11m) high. By the year 2000 the pile should reach 2,772 feet (831.6m).

Parchment Paradise

The government has been studying the proliferation of paperwork and found that it spends in excess of $15 million a year on paper. It's one thing to do the study and another to do something about the study.

So, the Paper Management Office tried to encourage government employees to cut down on paperwork by having an annual contest. Letters *(paper, of course)* were sent out to government agencies telling them how to enter the names of nominees "who have contributed significantly to the efficiency or cost reduction of Federal paperwork systems." The nominating procedures were described in a six-page *(paper)* prospectus.

Decadent Decorating

For the modest sum of $325,000, the quarters of the "official temporary residence of the Vice-President of the United States" were refurbished. This breaks down as:

- $15,300 for china and crystal
- $18,100 for carpeting
- $21,200 for silverware
- $26,400 for drapes
- $33,000 for miscellaneous items
- $41,000 for furniture
- $170,000 for the replacement of window air conditioners with central air.

Top-Secret Decorating

Nancy Reagan showed off her $1 million White House redecorating project to *Architectural Digest,* but forbade their letting the public see any of the photos.

All That Glitters . . .

The Director of the Office of Management and Budget–yes, Management and Budget–spent $611,623 to add gold trim to one medium-sized room in the old Executive Office Building, which is next door to the White House.

Wired!

The Rural Electrification Administration (REA) was established to loan money to bring telephone service into rural areas. By the 1950s, however, 96 percent of the country had been wired, so REA's job had been done. Instead of closing down shop, REA started making loans to nuclear power plants that later went bankrupt. Now the money is going:

- to provide touchtone telephones to Micronesia
- to run ski lifts in Vale and Aspen, Colorado
- for electricity that powers golf carts in Hilton Head, South Carolina.

No Business Like . . .

President Reagan said he wasn't fully informed about the Iran Arms deal–including an estimated $10 to $30 million that ultimately went to the opponents of the Sandinista government. He did have some good ideas about it, though, like when he called Ollie North to say, "This is going to make a great movie one day."

What About a Garage Sale?

The government spends between $250 million and $676 million on new furnishings each year. And this doesn't include expensive items, such as computer equipment.

GOVERNMENT EFFICIENCY

The government is trying to make itself more efficient. Is government efficiency an oxymoron? Let's see.

Knock-Knock! Anybody Home?

The National Reconnaissance Office is under construction near Dulles International Airport, in Virginia, with a price tag of $310 million. Just 30 miles away, members of the Senate Select Committee on Intelligence–yes, Intelligence–didn't know this cost, though this intelligence group authorized the project and was "overseeing" it.

This Does Not Compute

The Department of Defense (DOD) purchased over $200 billion in computer equipment, which worked out like this:

The accounting department paid contractors $750 million in a six-month period. And DOD wasn't able to define what goods and services they received for $41 million of that money.

DOD's computerized inventory system bought $30 billion—yes, billion *(it's not a typo)*—of spare parts that proved unnecessary.

The military operates 161 major accounting systems, many of which are incompatible. So, DOD relies on outside contractors to report when they're being overpaid.

Once the government buys computer equipment, it takes approximately 49 months *(that's over four years)* to install it. Since the computer industry is moving into a new generation of technology every 18 months, this means the government is continually buying outdated equipment. Private industry takes about one year to complete the purchase-to-installation cycle.

Mayor, Mayor on the Wall

The Minority Business Development Agency, a division of the Department of Commerce, awarded grants of $200,000 each year to the Lower Rio Grande Valley Conference of Mayors in southern Texas. After the first conference the Mayors deemed it useless and a waste of tax dollars. But the grants were renewed each year for four more years.

Another Government Gaffe

The Economic Development Administration, a division of the Department of Commerce, permitted local authorities to mismanage a federally funded revolving-door loan program. The program was intended to give grants to local areas to further economic development, increase incomes, and reduce unemployment. Instead, it hijacked jobs from one part of the country to another.

It cost $215 million.

Getting Something for Nothing

The Fish and Wildlife Service of the Department of the Interior mismanaged its payroll to the tune of $217 million. It continued to pay people who had left their jobs and granted overtime to people who were on vacation or away on personal leave.

Bookkeeping 101

The National Park Service, Division of the Department of the Interior, uses interesting accounting practices. It listed:

- a $350 dishwasher as a $700,000 asset
- a $150 vacuum cleaner as an $800,000 asset
- a fire truck as a 1-cent asset.

I Should Get My Two Cents Out of This One

Resolution Trust Corporation recently hired Price Waterhouse to copy documents belonging to HomeFed Savings Association at the cost of 67 cents a copy. If you multiply that by the 10 million pages that were copied, the cost came to $6.7 million. Many copy shops charge 2 cents a copy.

Also, in 1992 when the Federal Deposit Insurance Corporation and Resolution Trust were asking Congress for more tax dollars, an audit revealed that these agencies had spent $3,098 for thirty-six coffee mugs and twelve T-shirts, and $1,800 for two breast pumps.

To Bee or Not to Bee

The United States government pays out more than $95 million a year in subsidies. To name only a few—very few—there's the National Soft Drink Association, the National Swimming Pool Institute, the American Horse Council, the Tobacco Institute, as well as the Association of Beekeepers. *(By the way, beekeepers aren't beekeepers; they're honey processors.)*

Several honey processors were at the Rayburn Congressional Office Building in Washington to educate Congress on the needs of honey people. Questions and answers went like this:

Q. What sort of help do you honey processors need?
A. Well, insecticide poisoning often kills our colonies and stops production.
Q. Aren't you reimbursed for that?
A. Uh . . . Yes, we are.
Q. Have you personally gotten money from the government?
A. Uh . . . Yes, on several occasions.
Q. How much did you get?
A. Uh . . .
Q. How much did you get?
A. Uh . . .
Q. Okay, roughly how much did you get?
A. Roughly $500,000.

(Let's bee real here.)

ROLL IN THE RED CARPET

Florida Fiascos

What would be a better winter weekend for politicians than one spent in Florida–away from the punishing storms and brutal temperatures much of the country is experiencing–courtesy of lobbying groups, such as U.S. Tobacco and the insurance lobbyists. And it's not only the politicians who are getting the red carpet treatment. Lobbyists are so aimed at building relationships that they wine and dine not only congressional staffers, but also young administrative assistants.

ABC News cameras followed our congressional teams on such a trip to Florida's Gold Coast. The group was entertained at an exclusive Boca Raton resort and club. In one weekend, the tab was more than $150,000. Tennis pros, such as Ilie Nastasi and Roscoe Tanner, were brought in to play with the lawmakers.

Federal Frequent Flyer:
And the Winner Is...

John B. Breaux, Democratic Senator from Louisiana, has been on the congressional travel circuit. Lobbyists have paid for his trips to West Palm Beach, Fort Myers, Fort Walton Beach, Scottsdale, Palm Springs, Las Vegas, San Diego, and San Francisco. In his own defense, Senator Breaux said, "I don't select where they [the lobbyists] have conferences, they do."

4. Absurd Armed Forces

NAVAL NONSENSE

Orange Diplomas

The U.S. Naval Academy suffered from weeks of altercations. Members of the 1990 graduating class had cheated on exams and chained coeds to urinals as part of a hazing process. So, when they graduated, the Academy awarded them diplomas from the U.S. Navel Academy. *(A proofreading gaffe, of course!)*

More Padding
Than a Cushioned Toilet Seat

Remember when Maine Senator William Cohen and Delaware Senator William Roth announced that the Navy was paying $640 for a toilet seat that would cost us only $25? $400 for a hammer? $54 for a stapler, $50 of which is for paperwork. *(The trees are wincing.)*

Well, the National Aeronautics and Space Administration spent $23 million to build a prototype toilet for the space shuttle. The price tag represented a 900-percent increase over the original estimate, because the astronauts requested a manual flush rather than an automatic one.

How About Footing This Bill?

The United States Navy spent $792 for a designer doormat. The Navy is supposed to protect our seas so the enemy doesn't reach our doorstep, but this is going too far.

Spark Plugs

The U.S. Navy announced to the House Armed Services Oversight and Investigations Committee that it was paying $544.09 for a spark plug connector that could be bought off the shelf at hardware stores for $10.99. Adding sparks to this fire, the $544.09 connector required a five-month delivery period.

More Power To You

The Navy allotted $11.5 million to modernize the power plant at the Philadelphia Naval Yard. The plant had been scheduled to close.

This Is No Beach Party

The United States Navy wanted to improve its ship-to-ship communications, so it experimented with Frisbees to send messages. We haven't heard the dollar amount that was tossed away.

No More Bull

The Navy spent $10,000 on a study to determine the effect of naval communications on the potency of a bull.

THE AFFLUENT ARMY

Out on a Limb

The Department of the Army decided to use its surplus money to spruce up Fort Belvoir, Virginia, by planting decorative trees. The trees and shrubs died within a year and had to be uprooted. The landscape design cost $35,000 and the trees cost $124,000. We don't know the uprooting cost.

Making a Mountain Out of a Molehill

Have you ever played the game called "King of the Hill"? Each player strives to climb to the top of a hill and prevent all the other players from pushing him/her off. Well, the

U.S. Army spent $20,000 to produce 30,000 pamphlets explaining this game. The pamphlet contained:

- a preface
- four pages of detailed rules
- a multicolored diagram of an earthen mound.

Multiple Choice

Since 1946 the U.S. Army School of the Americas at Fort Benning, Georgia, has trained more than 56,000 Latin American soldiers. Among its graduates—whose educations we funded—were:

- Manuel Noriega, Class of '72: Voted "Most Likely to Succeed"
- Roberto d'Aubuisson, Class of '72: Managed Salvadoran death squads and ordered the assassination of a Catholic bishop while conducting Mass.

Since 1991, as a result of the atrocities of these grads, the school has mandated that students participate in a four-hour program on human rights. Here is one of the questions the students must answer:

SCENARIO: The squad leader gives an order to cut off the ears of dead enemy soldiers as proof of the number of casualties. You should:

a. Obey the order but denounce it to your superiors.
b. Obey the order.
c. Disobey the order and tell your superiors.
d. Order a squad member of lower rank to obey the order.

PENTAGON PRANKS

No News Might Be Good News

The Pentagon spends $162 million a year to produce and buy periodicals and newspapers, though it admits that most of them are nonessential and that many are repetitious. The Department of Defense spends $20.4 million for much of the same stuff. Each branch of the military, being a separate entity, wants its own publications.

What's Cooking at the Pentagon?

After a six-month study, the Pentagon released its 22-page official brownie recipe. Here are some excerpts:

- The texture of the brownie shall be firm but not hard.
- Pour batter into a pan at a rate that will yield uncoated brownies which, when cut such as to meet the dimension requirements specified in regulation 3.4f, will weigh approximately 35 grams each.
- The dimensions of the coated brownie shall not exceed 3½ inches by 2½ inches by ⅝ inch.
- Shelled walnut pieces shall be of the small piece size classification, shall be of a light color, and shall be U.S. No. 1 of the U.S. Standards for Shelled English Walnuts. A minimum of 90 percent, by weight, of the pieces shall pass through a 4/16-inch-diameter round-hole screen and not more than 1 percent, by weight, shall pass through a 2/16-inch-diameter round-hole screen.

And here's what it had to say about the proper pumpkin pie filling:

Good consistency means that the canned pumpkin . . . after emptying from the container to a dry-flat surface . . . holds high mound formation, and at the end of ten minutes after emptying on such surface, the highest point of the mound is not less than 60 percent of the height of the container.

Lottery, Anyone?

In 1989 Congress authorized the Pentagon to spend $49,000 to determine if members of the armed forces would buy military lottery tickets.

Barely Acceptable

The taxpayers paid the salary of a senior Naval officer who had female Navy civilian employees pose nude for photographs. He claimed the photographs would be used for a series of training posters on board ships that were deployed to the Persian Gulf during the Gulf War. The shots were a cleaning sequence that started with routine deck scrubbing to wet T-shirts to more revealing poses. A favorite of many wives who posed was a "housecleaning, laundry, kitchen work sequence designed to emphasize their hard work at home." The good news is that the captain was charged with conduct unbecoming an officer. He was fined $1,000 and asked to resign.

Tell It to the Tooth Fairy

The Pentagon spent $2,000 to bury the tooth of Army Warrant Officer Gregory S. Crandall at Arlington National Cemetery. Crandall's dog tags had been found in 1971, and it was assumed that his helicopter crashed in Laos. The tooth was buried in a full-sized casket with full military honors. Crandall's family was appalled and attended under protest. The family sent out announcements that read: "The family of Warrant Officer Gregory S. Crandall regrets to announce the burial of a single tooth as his remains at Arlington National Cemetery on September 17 at 1:00. Your attendance is welcome."

No 20/20 Vision

Using the code name "Star Gate," the Pentagon has spent more than $20 million to employ psychics to pursue the unknown. The Pentagon hoped these crystal-ball gazers would give the Defense Intelligence Agency a paranormal advantage. According to David Goslin of the American Institute for Research, "There's no documented evidence that it [the psychic program] had any value to the intelligence community." For example, in 1981, when an American general, James Dozier was kidnapped, one psychic told the Pentagon that he was being held in Italy, in a stone house with a red roof. Well, that accounts for most Italian homes!

Family Feud

Don't we have anything better to do now that the Cold War is over? We spent $150,000 to study the feud between the Hatfields and the McCoys.

Bad Hair Day

Male members of the Army are prohibited from carrying umbrellas to the Pentagon on a rainy day. However, female members of the Army can use umbrellas, and so can members of the Air Force and the Navy.

AIR FORCE ANTICS

Just the Fax, Ma'am

The Air Force spent $94.6 million to buy 173 fax machines designed by Litton Industries. These fax machines cost $547,000 each but will survive nuclear blasts. Senator Carl Levin, Democrat from Michigan, found out that the Air Force had rejected fax machines built by Magnavox that cost only $15,000 each.

Tools of the Trade

Pratt & Whitney told the Air Force it needed pliers to modify engines on F-111 aircraft. The contractor hired a subcontractor to build the pliers for $669.00 each. The subcontractor then added in $330.20 in overhead and profit. Thus, each pair of pliers cost $999.20.

Quail Cuisine

The government spent $22,000 and used military aircraft to fly two Air Force officials to Washington, DC, for a quail breakfast. It was a purely social engagement.

Just Horsing Around

In 1990 the U.S. Air Force bestowed upon the University of Florida a $100,000 grant to see if the noise of low-flying F-4 Phantom fighter jets would have a negative affect on pregnant horses in the Southwest.

5. Food and Fun

FUNKY FOOD

Soaring with Eagles and Trucking with Turkeys

A month before Thanksgiving in 1993, the Department of Agriculture launched unannounced inspections of turkey processing plants and issued the results after Thanksgiving. "If you're going to put out warnings or tell the results of the inspection," reasoned Representative John Mica, Republican from Florida, "wouldn't it be wise to do it prior to the season when you have the highest consumption?"

Comparing Apples and Oranges

How often have you heard combatants try to clarify their points of view by blurting out, "You're comparing apples to oranges." Well, the National Aeronautics and Space Administration thought it was worth looking into this.

It sponsored a team from Ames Research Center, Moffett Field, California, which compared Granny Smith Apples and Sunkist Navel Oranges. The team dried these fruits in a convection oven at low temperature over the course of a few days. They then mixed them with potassium bromide and ground them in a mill. One hundred milligrams of the powders were then pressed into a circular pellet. The findings?

Apples and oranges are very similar.

(This should have a striking effect on future arguments.)

Treats Are Where You Find Them

Rats had a feast eating the insides of a $93,000 Xerox machine in the Cannon House Office Building. When the machine was opened up to find out why it wasn't working, an employee discovered that inside the Xerox machine there were banana peels, corncobs, and a Hostess Twinkie still sealed in its plastic wrapping. With a $10,000 trade-in, a replacement machine cost the taxpayers an additional $97,000.

RECKLESS RECREATION

Money Down the Drain

Over $1 million was given to Trenton, New Jersey, for a sewer line so it could bypass a 100-year-old sewer that had been declared a landmark. This historic landmark is a brick-lined sewer that's 25 feet underground. It has been visited by only two people in 23 years.

This Is a Backhanded Shot

The National Endowment for the Arts spent $2,500 to find out why people are rude and ill-mannered on the tennis court. The outcome of this study is unknown, but it won its approval in Faquier and Rappahannock counties, Virginia. Its purpose was to solve the problem of people having to wait hours for court time, and getting them to understand that there wasn't enough money in local budgets to build additional courts. The recipient of this Golden Fleece Award, Helen Sweeney, director of Arlington's Williamsburg recreation district, said about the award: "I'm perplexed, but I'm enjoying it."

The Wave of the Future?

"Federal Bureaucrats Make Waves and the Taxpayer Gets Soaked." This headline ushered in an historic moment. The Bureau of Outdoor Recreation of the Department of the Interior spent $145,000 to install a surf-making machine in a double-Olympic-sized swimming pool in Salt Lake City. The rationale? A spokesman for the project claimed that "Residents will no longer need to jump in their campers and travel 300 miles to feel the rushing water of Flaming Gorge."

Up the Creek Without a Paddle

The Bureau of Housing and Urban Development bestowed over $1 million on Pittsburgh, Pennsylvania, for building an access road, ramp, and tunnel to a private entertainment spa. This was to include sightseeing and shuttle boats, and a three-tiered floating dock. What's so odd about that?

- The passenger boat ended up in New York.
- The whereabouts of the shuttle is unknown.
- The dock emerged as two barges.

Sandbagging Us All?

Imagine the U.S. Army Corps of Engineers spending $33 million to pump sand onto ten miles of beach in Miami, Florida. This will probably add to the pleasures of those who stay in the condominiums and hotels. But geologists expect that Miami Beach will eventually become the Miami seawall. The Corps has talked about starting work on another 2.5 miles because "local interests desire extension to the northern limit." What's the limit? Palm Beach? Virginia Beach? Bar Harbor?

The Joker's Wild

The Department of the Air Force spent $59,000 for decks of cards that were given as souvenirs to visitors aboard Air Force Two. *(Does it make you wonder if the Executive Office is playing with a full deck?)*

This Is a Bat-ty One

Imagine spending $100,000 to construct a 100-foot baseball bat. The Works Progress Administration didn't just imagine it–they did it! If anyone finds a use for this bat, please let me know.

Absolutely Wreck-reational

Are rock concerts, golf balls, and health club memberships vital to our national security? Well, auditors for the Department of Defense have blown the whistle on Martin Marietta and its subsidiaries for charging the government:

- $263,000 for a Smokey Robinson concert in Denver, Colorado
- $20,194 for professional-quality golf balls
- $17,487 for softball and volleyball games.

Another unnamed contractor submitted a bill for $144,000 for health club memberships and $55,000 for tea and coffee.

6. It's All in the Delivery

ASININE ADVERTISING

Return to Sender

Over $137,000 of our tax dollars sent 85 postal executives to a tennis resort south of Orlando, Florida. The intent was to prepare them for improved delivery of the Christmas mail. The curriculum included classroom and outdoor training on 30-foot poles and rope ladders designed to give obstinate managers a "breakthrough experience."

It Pays to Advertise

Can U.S. Savings Bonds be sold in the same way as bras and automobiles? The answer is probably yes, because the Federal Government was ranked 28th by the magazine *Advertising Age* on its annual list of the nation's 100 leading advertisers. In one year alone, the government gave more than $228,857,200.00 to the admen. In that same year Proctor & Gamble spent $773,818,300.00 and Sears spent $732,500,000.00.

"Ad" This to the List

As part of its "Market Promotion Program," Uncle Sam picks up the tab for billions of advertising dollars. Our Uncle surely has his favorite nieces and nephews:

- $5.1 million was given to Gallo Wines.
- $1.1 million was given to Tyson Chickens.
- $1 million was given to Ocean Spray.
- $6.2 million was given to Blue Diamond Almonds. *(Is that nuts?)*
- $465,000 was given to McDonald's.

We're also picking up the tab for over $70 million given to Sunkist to help them advertise overseas the oranges we're not allowed to buy in the United States.

Beauty Is Only Skin Deep

However, it digs deep into our pockets too. Look at what it cost to renovate the House Beauty Salon–$350,000.

MUDDLED MAIL

Keep Those Cards and Letters Rollin'

The U.S. Postal Service spent $3.4 million on a Madison Avenue ad campaign to persuade us to write more letters. A spokesperson for the Postal Service claimed that its purpose was to increase the volume of mail. Low volume is one of the causes of the agency's chronic deficit. Then they spent $775,000 more to see if the campaign was working. The answer hasn't been disclosed.

Winning Losses

In 1993 the Post Office lost $500 million, which was $215 million over the losses that were expected. Shortly thereafter, Postmaster General Marvin Runyon announced large cash bonuses for his top managers if they could keep the losses to $1.3 million. Are we paying bonuses for losses?

No-go Logo

Also in 1993, while the Post Office laid off 30,000 workers in an effort to cut costs, it spent $7 million to replace its logo. Runyon justified this expense by saying that it represented a "clean break with our bureaucratic past."

Indoor Plumbing

The manager of a Chicago post office exercised "poor judgment," according to officials, when she spent $200,000 to have a bathroom and kitchen renovated. Prior to the time the renovation started, the post office was slated to move to a new site one block away.

Who Said There's No Free Parking?

The Treasury Postal Service spent $2.4 million for the construction of a parking lot that would provide 200 parking spaces for federal employees. There were only 18 federal employees in the facility.

IS THERE LIFE AFTER APRIL 15TH?

No Reverence

The son of John Zwynenburg was one of the tragic victims of Pan Am Flight 103 in 1988. The Internal Revenue Service guesstimated that the Zwynenburg family would be awarded over $11 million for their son's death and gave the bereaved family 90 days to pay taxes on that amount of money, even though no settlement had been reached.

Under Protest

Brooklyn retiree John McCormick sent a check to the Internal Revenue Service (IRS) with his tax return. Underneath his signature he wrote the words "under protest." The IRS slapped him with a penalty of $500. There were no inaccuracies in his return; this was a flagrant fine. Mr. McCormick went to court because the First Amendment of the Constitution "protects the right of protest to any branch of government." Apparently this doesn't apply to the IRS, because the judge ruled against this retiree.

IRS Compensation

In 1992 the Internal Revenue Service overpaid $20 billion in Earned Income Tax Credit to people who hadn't even applied. This program was designed to help workers poor enough for welfare, but 90 percent of the benefit checks went to people like aliens and prisoners who have no income at all.

Murphy's Law of Computers

The IRS was trying to collect $2 million in back taxes from Joseph H. Hale, who was serving time in a federal prison. Instead, the IRS issued him a check for $359,380.25. Two years later the IRS had recovered $55,558.34 of the money. It seemed that Hale had a friend who helped him dispose of the rest.

7. Citizen Beware

GUILTY WHEN PROVEN INNOCENT

Can you believe that federal agents can use your tax dollars to seize your home, wallet, car, and other possessions, even if you are completely innocent of any crime? If you want to get your property back, you have to post a bond equal to 10 percent of the value of your property. This is to cover the government's costs in defending itself against you. And it can cost you tens of thousands of dollars in your own legal fees to recoup your possessions.

Anonymous Call

In East Hartland, Connecticut, agents seized the home of Walter and Joann Cwikla because they had received an anonymous call that the Cwiklas were storing a small amount of marijuana. Federal agents never even searched the home; they merely confiscated it and nailed a notice on the front door declaring that the property had been seized. After five years and $25,000 in legal fees, this couple is still trying to reclaim their home.

Sweater Girl

An Iowa woman was accused of stealing a $25 sweater. Shortly thereafter agents confiscated her $18,000 car that was specially equipped to transport her handicapped daughter. They claimed that the vehicle was used as the getaway car.

Gray Druggies

In 1991, agents raided the Utah home of an elderly couple named Robert and Vera Garcia. The agents confiscated their home, their retirement savings, and a few hundred dollars in cash. The agents claimed that all the Garcias' possessions were purchased with drug money. No evidence was ever found to substantiate this, and the agents have offered no evidence to justify that seizure. However, the Garcias have had none of their property returned.

To the Victor . . .

Here are two of countless examples showing how confiscated assets are being spent:

- Officers in Greensboro, North Carolina, used seized loot to pay for equipment for an exercise room for themselves.
- In Erie County, New York, confiscated money was used by the sheriff to buy himself a snappy red Ford Crown Victoria car. A similar purchase was made in Suffolk County, New York—only that agent bought a BMW. *(The color wasn't mentioned.)*

UNCATEGORICALLY UNREASONABLE

"Why Do Fools Fall in Love?"

This "love story" was the recipient of the first Golden Fleece Award. The National Science Institute wanted to find out why and for how long males and females are attracted to each other. The cost of this fiscal fling? $84,000. *(Can anyone tell us the results?)*

Challenged!

The Equal Employment Opportunity Commission (EEOC) ruled that obesity is protected under the Americans with Disabilities Act (ADA) of 1990. Southwest Airline was sued by a 400-pound woman when an agent allegedly asked the woman to purchase two seats.

The ADA forced the owner of the Odd Ball Cabaret, a strip joint, to close one of its dancing stalls, because the stall wasn't accessible to a stripper in a wheelchair.

The ADA brought charges against a company that refused to hire a man who claimed he had a microchip in one of his teeth, which allowed him to communicate with people far, far away.

A lawyer for the EEOC implied that companies must exercise extreme caution when they discipline employees who attack their supervisors. Why? Because the employee may have a mental disability, which the company must accommodate.

Can't See the Forest for the Trees

The U.S. Forest Service was severely criticized because it wasn't hiring enough women as firefighters. Their reasoning was that women weren't strong enough to lug the heavy firefighting equipment. When the Equal Employment Opportunity Commission got on its case, the Forest Service placed a job announcement stating that "Only unqualified applicants may apply." A second announcement stated that "Only applicants who do not meet [job requirement] standards will be considered."

It's What's Up Front That Counts

The U.S. Bureau of Alcohol, Tobacco, and Firearms (BATF) recently banned one brand of Italian wine, Collio, because the bottles displayed bosomy naked women. So Collio began shipping bottles with flat-chested naked women, and BATF did not object. Dot Koester, spokesperson for the agency, said, "There is nothing objectionable about being perfectly flat-chested. The label is like seeing a man at the beach."

A Sense of Community

Once upon a time in a small community near Merrill Township, Michigan, the Bureau of Housing and Urban Development (HUD) approved $279,000 to build a community center for counseling, distributing food stamps, and conducting literacy classes and job training. The site selected was secluded in a virtually inaccessible forest.

Funds were not sufficient to complete a road to the site, so a partial road was built that did not reach anywhere near the community center. The road extended far enough to permit walkers to get to a narrow path, which ended in a pile of rubble. Without a road leading to the center, the project literally collapsed, but HUD never even knew it. So, there sits an inaccessible, unused community center built in the middle of nowhere.

Jailhouse Rock

The Law Enforcement Assistance Administration spent $27,000 to determine why inmates escape from jail. The real crime here was spending money for the study.

"I Do" or "I Don't"

Spent by the National Science Foundation to study the role of non-marriage in rural Irish families–$28,578. Apparently, Ireland has one of the highest rates of late and non-marriage. *(Does the NSF think the Irish know something that we don't?)*

MEDICAL MANIA

Supervigilant!

The Food and Drug Administration might be going a bit far. It has been trying to govern the distribution of sunglasses and frames, a wheelchair cushion, a dental bib, a low-pressure mattress, and a foot comfort massager.

Sign on the Dotted Line

The Food and Drug Administration (FDA) has refused to approve a pump that can save the life of heart attack victims. This device has been so successful in Austria and France that it is mandatory equipment on ambulances in those two countries. Why is the FDA refusing? The agency insists that the pump makers get the "informed consent" of any patient on whom the pump is tested. That's not very likely to happen, because at the point that this pump would be effective, the victims are clinically dead.

Utter Nun-Sense

The National Institute of Health spent over $1 million to explore the incidents of cervical cancer in women. For this study, two groups of women were used: nuns who were virgins and "nuns who are sexually active." *(I wonder how many volunteered for the second group?)*

"X" Marks the Spot

The National Institute of Neurological and Communicative Disorders and Stroke conducted a study to determine whether someone can place a hex on an opponent during a strength endurance test by drawing an "X" on the front of his opponent's chest. What a boon this could be for the 98-pound weakling! The Institute tried to justify this $160,000 expense with the following statement:

"The phenomenon under investigation cannot be understood or explained by information currently available and it is of obvious interest to determine what other heretofore unknown factors or mechanisms significantly influence muscle strength and movement."

All Washed Up

In 1993 the Environmental Protection Agency initiated a study into the hazards of breathing while taking a shower.

They were specifically interested in seeing whether a person might be harmed by inhaling water vapor.

How I Spent My Summer Vacation ... in Beverly Hills Learning About Poor Children

The Centers for Disease Control and Prevention (CDCP) spent $1,015,900 on a posh gathering of 238 employees at the Century Plaza Hotel in Beverly Hills, California, to discuss problems involved in vaccinating low-income children. House Health and Environmental Subcommittee Chairman Scott Klug, Democrat from Wisconsin, estimated that the amount of money spent on these employees could have immunized 13,500 children. *(Is this germ welfare?)*

A Hare-Raising Experience

In 1993 the Physicians' Committee for Responsible Medicine spent $3 million to determine if marijuana could make rabbits more prone to syphilis and mice more prone to Legionnaire's disease.

Use It Or Lose It

When $122 million was allocated for an addition to the Dirksen Office Building in Washington, DC, it went to give the senators a third gymnasium. *(Can't they jog or power walk like the rest of us?)*

8. Mixed Messages

ERRONEOUS EDUCATION

Boob-Tubing

The Department of Education spent $219,000 to teach college students how to watch television effectively. *(Given the hours that the average American watches television, what's to be learned?)*

Send a Lawyer to Camp?

Should doctors, lawyers, and school administrators get away for free summer vacations? *Free* summer vacations? The National Endowment for the Humanities feels it's imperative "to broaden and sharpen their perspectives."

Lowdown Louisiana

Another Golden Fleece Award winner . . . According to an audit prepared by the Inspector General of the Department of Education, DOE fleeced the taxpayers for $912,678 by allowing education officials in Louisiana to divert money earmarked for handicapped children. Instead of providing for the needs of these children, $385,200 was spent on computer projects for the general student population. Inexperienced and noncertified personnel approved this three-year-long ripoff and paid for a staff person to work nine months, when in fact the person worked only six weeks.

My Oh Mayan

Do you speak Tzotzil? Do you know people who speak Tzotzil? If you answer yes to either of these questions, perhaps you can figure out how the Smithsonian Institution can justify spending $89,000 to produce a Tzotzil dictionary.

About 120,000 Mayan descendants, peasants in a corn-farming town in southern Mexico, speak Tzotzil, an unwritten—yes, *unwritten*–language.

Research Grants

Universities receive billions of dollars each year to conduct research. But how far does research extend? Let's examine the research of Stanford University. It spent:

- $7,000 for sheets to cover the enlarged bed of the dean
- $1,000 a month to wash the dean's laundry
- $1,500 for liquor for pre-football game parties, etc.

Other universities, such as Rutgers, Yale, Duke, Emory, Johns Hopkins, and MIT, were earmarking funds for trips to Europe and the Caribbean, artwork, foreign language lessons, storytelling for Christmas functions, sabbaticals, and golf club memberships—all in the name of learning. *(What lessons are to be learned here?)*

All in the Name of Learning

The following universities billed the government for these expenses:

- Dartmouth College—$20,490 to chauffeur the president of the college and his wife
- Massachusetts Institute of Technology—$4,655 for its contribution to the Museum of Fine Arts
- Cornell University—$1,000 for a Steuben glass and wine goblet
- Stanford University—$3,000 for a cedar-lined closet, and $2,000 for monthly deliveries of flowers to the home of the university president.

Rock 'n' Roll

The National Institute of Education spent $900,000 to buy a disco and promote a rock concert.

ABSURD AGRICULTURE

Here's Egg in Your Face

The United States Department of Agriculture performed a study to see how long it takes to fry eggs in a skillet. After spending $46,000, we know it takes 838 time measurement units (TMUs). *(Was that over easy or sunnyside up?)*

Down on the Farm

The Environmental Protection Agency spent over $38,000 to determine if the runoff from open stacks of cow manure on farms in Vermont was causing pollution in water in near-by streams and ponds.

The Old Bamboo

The Department of Agriculture spent $63,000 on bamboo research. None grows in the U.S.

How Long Can It Last?

This can only happen in the federal fertilizer factory, which is the National Fertilizer Development Center in Muscle Shoals, Alabama. During World War II the plant was designed to produce nitrate to be used in munitions. The government no longer needs the fertilizer, but it still donates $20 million a year to this plant.

The CONnecticut Con (aka Manure-Gate)

Would you consider Fairfield County, Connecticut–one of the wealthiest suburbs of New York City–to be a farm in need of government aid? Back in the 1930s it was, but not anymore. This area, however, still has farm status according to the Department of Agriculture (DOA). Therefore, the Oxbridge Hunt Club–where it costs $20,000 to board your horse–is given money by DOA to help build a dock to haul off their manure.

This Is a Meaty One

The Department of Agriculture spent $90,000 to study the "behavioral determinants of vegetarianism."

LOCATION, LOCATION, LOCATION

Playground of the Rich and Famous

The Bureau of Housing and Urban Development has also placed welfare families on the expensive island of Nantucket, Massachusetts. HUD is paying in the neighborhood of $1,750 a month for apartments to house these folks.

In the Lap of Luxury

You may not be rich enough to live next door to Hollywood celebs, but you certainly may be poor enough.

Housing and Urban Development is spending about $8 million to house 28 welfare families in the middle of one of California's most expensive seaside neighborhoods. The "La Jolla Villas" will offer subsidized rents starting at $323 a month in an area where a mid-priced home can go for a half million. In addition to an ocean view, each welfare family will also have its dues paid for the local country club. This tab is $310 per month per family, for an additional $104,160.

Mel Shapiro, local housing rights activist, values this land at $2.5 million. He expressed his disgust when he said, "I'm a housing advocate, not an idiot."

What's the Resale Value?

In 1986 the National Park Service bought a half acre of land in southwest Washington, DC, for the price of $230,000. Two years later a search showed that the National Park Service had already owned the land. It had purchased that same parcel in 1914.

Icy Finding

What was the climate like in Africa during the last Ice Age? Cold. It took $121,000 of our tax dollars to find that out.

HOLE-Y MACKEREL

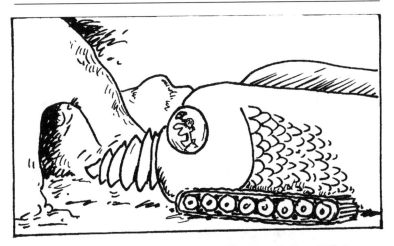

Someone Should Be WIPP-ed for This

The U.S. Department of Energy has dug a big hole in the ground called the Waste Isolation Pilot Plan (WIPP). It was supposed to be America's trash dump for low-level, non-toxic waste. This seven-mile tunnel, which stretches a half mile underground, was finished in 1989. But with changing regulations and lawsuits, it still isn't open.

Meanwhile, it costs more than $7 million a year to maintain it. That brings the cost to more than $2 billion, since the project started in the 70's. Even though WIPP isn't opened, it employs:

- 45 people to keep nuclear records *(There are no records to keep.)*
- elevator operators *(Who's being lifted and lowered?)*
- guards *(What are they guarding? Their lunch?)*
- a public relations staff of over 2,000 *(It sounds more like private relations, not public.)*

WIPP has been criticized by its own proponents, who claim that with better management the government could have saved the taxpayers more than $400 million from 1989 to 1994. If the plant is to open, another $1.5 million needs to be poured into the hole.

Operating in the Hole

The Department of Labor's Mine Safety and Health Administration (MSHA) is supposed to recover the entire cost of equipment testing by passing the charges along to the manufacturer of the equipment. But it seems MSHA didn't charge the manufacturers enough. The expenses to the taxpayers mounted to a $10 million tab.

More Waste (Literally)

In Yucca Mountain, Nevada, the Department of Energy (DOE) wanted to store the nation's nuclear waste and decided to build a repository for that purpose. In order to dig the tunnel, DOE bought a 25-foot tunnel-boring machine that cost $13 million. The government already owned an 18-foot boring machine that would have been more than adequate to dig the tunnel.

DOE was advised by its technical review board that if it bought the bigger machine, it would have to buy a special conveyor belt that would cost another $2.25 million. So, DOE is back on Capitol Hill asking for the additional $2.25 million, while the 25-foot tunnel-boring machine is tunneling along, slowly and inefficiently.

WACKY WASTERS
HALL OF FAME

Animal and Plant Health Inspection Service
Bureau of Alcohol, Tobacco, and Firearms
Centers for Disease Control and Prevention
Comprehensive Employment and Training Act
Department of Agriculture
Department of Commerce
Department of Defense
Department of Education
Department of Energy
Department of the Interior
Department of Labor
Department of Transportation
Environmental Protection Agency
Equal Employment Opportunity Commission

Federal Aviation Administration
Federal Highway Administration
Federal Home Administration
Food and Drug Administration
Food and Nutrition Services
General Accounting Office
Government Service Administration
Housing and Urban Development
Internal Revenue Service
Minority Business Development Agency
Mine Safety and Health Administration
National Aeronautics and Space Administration
National Endowment for the Arts
National Endowment for the Humanities
National Fertilizer Development Center
National Highway Traffic Safety Administration
National Institute of Alcohol Abuse and Alcoholism
National Institute of Education
National Institute of Health
National Institute of Mental Health
National Institute of Neurological and Communicative
    Disorder and Stroke
National Institute of Standards and Technology
National Oceanic and Atmospheric Administration
National Reconnaissance Office
National Science Foundation
National Science Institute
Office of Management and Budget
Pentagon
Resolution Trust Corporation
Rural Electrification Administration
Small Business Administration
Smithsonian Institution
Urban Mass Transit Administration
United States Armed Forces
United States Department of Agriculture

About the Author

SHERYL LINDSELL-ROBERTS is a well-known and highly respected author who's been writing books for the professional market for the last fifteen years. Her first entree into the humor market was with Sterling's hot seller, *Loony Laws and Silly Statutes.* Sheryl has received national acclaim for *Loony Laws* on nationwide talk shows and in *Woman's Day,* the *Sun,* the *National Enquirer,* and *Entrepreneur* magazines.

Sheryl and her husband, Jon, live in "Parnassus," the beautiful home they recently built in Marlborough, Massachusetts. She enjoys traveling (especially visiting her sons, Marc and Eric, in California), photographing nature, skiing, and sailing *Worth th' Wait.*

About the Illustrator

MYRON MILLER, the cartoonist and illustrator, lives in Westport, Connecticut, without any grants.

Index

Accounting practices, 43
Administration, 14
Advertising, 66-68
Africa, 88
Agriculture, 85-86
Air Force, 57-58
Air Force Two, 64
Airplanes, 18-20
Alcohol, 26, 27
American Institute for Research, 56
Americans with Disabilities Act, 75, 76
Ames Research Center, 61
Animals, 25-34
Apples and oranges, 61
Architectural Digest, 39
Armed Forces, 47-58
Attraction, 75
Bamboo, 86
Baseball bat, 64
Bathroom and kitchen, 69
Beagles, 30
Beekeepers, 33, 44
Blackbirds, 32
Blomquist, Gary, 34
Blue Diamond Almonds, 67
Breathing, 80
Breaux, John B., 46
Bridges, 14-15
Brownie recipe, 54
Bull, potency of, 50
Bullfights, 30
Bureau of Alcohol, Tobacco, and Firearms, 76
Bureau of Land Management, 14
Bureau of Outdoor Recreation, 63
Buses, 14
Bush, George, 17
Business travel, 17
Cannon House Office Building, 61
Canoe, 8
Catfish, 37
Census, 27

Centers for Disease Control and Prevention, 80
Chambersburg, Pennsylvania, 13
Chauffeur services, 13, 15
Children: handicapped, 83; vaccinating, 80
Cockroaches, 31
Cohen, William, 49
Collio wine, 76
Community Center, Merrill Township, Michigan, 77
Comprehensive Employment and Training Act, 27
Computer equipment, 42
Concerts, rock, 64, 84
Confiscated assets, 74
Cooking, 54
Cornell University, 84
Cow manure, 85
Cows, belching, 31
Crandall, Gregory S., 55
Cwikla, Walter and Joann, 73
d'Aubuisson, Roberto, 52
Dartmouth College, 84
Decoration, government, 39, 40
Department of Agriculture, 29, 60, 85, 86
Department of Commerce, 42
Department of Defense, 20, 37, 42, 53, 64
Department of Education, 82, 83
Department of Energy, 89, 90
Department of Labor, 90
Department of the Army, 51, 52
Department of the Air Force, 64
Department of the Interior, 27, 30, 43, 63
Department of Transportation, 24
Dirksen Office Building, 80

Disabilities, 76
Disneyworld, 23
Doormat, designer, 49
Dozier, Gen. James, 56
Earned Income Tax Credit, 71
Earthquakes, 37
Economic Development Administration, 42
Eggs, frying, 85
Endangered Species Act, 27
Environmental Protection Agency, 31, 79, 85
Equal Employment Opportunity Commission, 75, 76
F4-Phantom fighter jets, 58
Fax machines, 57
Federal Aviation Administration, 19, 20, 21
Federal Deposit Insurance Corporation, 43
Federal Highway Administration, 14
Federal Home Administration, 12
Feeney, Brian, 21-22
Fertilizer, 86
Feud, Hatfields and McCoys, 56
Firefighters, women, 76
Fish, 26
Fish and Wildlife Service, 27, 43
Flatulence, cow, 8
Florida airports, 19
Florida, University of, 58
Food and Nutrition Services
Food, 59-61
Food and Drug Administration, 19, 78
Foreign governments, 35-37
Fort Belvoir, Virginia, 51
Fort Benning, Georgia, 52
Fort Worth Regional Office of Urban Mass Transportation, 14

Frisbees, 50
Gallo Wines, 67
Games, 62-64
Garcia, Robert and Vera, 74
Gas emissions, 8
General Accounting Office
General Services Administration, 16
Global warming, 31
Golden Fleece Award, 9, 13, 14, 19, 63, 75, 83
Goslin, David, 56
Government Service Administration
Gymnasium, Senate, 80
Hale, Joseph H., 71
Harvard Medical School, 28
Hawaiian canoe, 8
Health club memberships, 64
Helistat, 19
Hellgate Viaduct, 14
Hex, 79
Honey processors, 44
Honking, 13
Horses, pregnant, 58
House Armed Services Oversight and Investigations Committee, 49
House Beauty Salon, 67
Houseflies, 34
Housing, welfare, 87-88
Housing and Urban Development, 13, 63, 77, 87
Hutchins, Daniel, 22
Ice Age, 88
Internal Revenue Service, 70-71
Iran Arms deal, 40
Irish marriages, 77
Jail, why inmates escape from, 77
Japanese: government, 37; quail, 33
Jason and the Golden Fleece, 9
King of the Hill, 51
Klug, Rep. Scott, 80
Koester, Dot, 76-77
La Jolla Villas, 88

Law Enforcement Assistance Administration, 77
Legionnaire's disease, 80
Levin, Sen. Carl, 57
Light bulb, 13
Limousine, most expensive, 13
Litton Industries, 57
Lobbyists, 45-46
Logo, post office, 69
Lottery tickets, military, 54
Manure, cow, 85
Marijuana, 73, 80
Market Promotion Program, 67
Martin Marietta, 64
Massachusetts Institute of Technology, 84
Mayors, Conference of, 42
McCormick, John, 71
McDade, Joseph M., 17
McDonald's, 67
McKinley, Mt., 8
Miami, Florida, beach, 63-64
Mica, Rep. John, 60
Mice, 80
Mine Safety and Health Administration, 90
Minority Business Development Agency, 42
Monkeys, 27
Moroccan Embassy, 37
Mosquito Creek, 14
Motorcycle, back-steering, 13
National Archives, 38
National Aeronautics and Space Administration, 27, 49, 61
National Endowment for the Arts, 19, 62-63
National Endowment for the Humanities, 82
National Fertilizer Development Center, 86
National Highway Traffic Safety Administration, 13
National Institute of Alcohol Abuse and Alcoholism, 26, 27
National Institute of Education, 84

National Institute of Health, 79
National Institute of Mental Health, 33, 36
National Institute of Neurological and Communicative Disorder and National Institute of Standards and Technology
National Oceanic and Atmospheric Administration, 20
National Park Service, 43, 88
National Reconnaissance Office, 41
National Science Foundation, 13, 27, 30, 31, 32, 33, 34, 77
National Science Institute, 75
Navy, U.S., 48-50
Newspapers, 53
Noriega, Manuel, 52
North, Ollie, 40
Nude photographs, 55
Nuns, 79
Obesity, 75
Ocean Spray, 67
Odd Ball Cabaret, 76
Office of Naval Research, 27
Office of Management and Budget, 39
Oxbridge Hunt Club, 86
Paper, waste of, 38-39, 49
Paper Management Office, 38
Parishes, Louisiana, 8
Parking lot, 69
Payroll mismanagement, 43
Penguins, overweight, 30
Pentagon, 53-56
Periodicals, 53
Philadelphia Naval Yard, 49
Photographs, nude, 55
Physicians' Committee for Responsible Medicine, 80
Pierce, Jr., Samuel R., 13
Pigeon economics, 32
Pigs, pregnant, 29

Pliers, 58
Pollution, 85
Pratt & Whitney, 58
Price Waterhouse, 43
Proctor & Gamble, 67
Prostitutes, 36-37
Proxmire, Sen. William, 9
Psychics, 55-56
Puerto Rico trips, 18
Pump, life-saving, 78-79
Pumpkin pie filling recipe, 54
Pyramid, Great, 8
Quail, Japanese, 33
Rabbits, 80
Rats, 27, 61
Reagan, Nancy, 39
Reagan, Ronald, 40
Research grants, 83
Resolution Trust Corporation, 43
Resolution Trust Corporation, 43
Restroom, 8
Roads, 12-15
Roth, William, 49
Runyon, Postmaster General Marvin, 69
Rural Electrification Administration, 40
Sand pumping, 63-64
Sears, 67
Senate Select Committee on Intelligence, 41
Sexual behavior, 33, 34, 75

Shapiro, Mel, 88
Shuler, John, 27
Smithsonian Institute, 83
Smokey the Bear, 34
Snakes, brown tree, 30
Southwest Airline, 75
Spark plug connector, 49
Special Airlift Mission, 18
Stamps, 7
Stanford University, 83-84
Star Gate, 55-56
Steamtown National Historic Site Museum, 17
Stripper in wheelchair, 76
Stroke, 79
Subsidies, 44
Subway rides, 17
Sunkist, 67
Surf-making machine, 63
Sweeney, Helen, 63
Syphilis, 80
Taxes, 70-71
Television, how to watch, 82
Tennis resort, 66
Tennis court rudeness, 62-63
Thanksgiving, 60
Time Measurement Units (TMUs), 85
Toilet, space shuttle, 49
Tourist attractions. 17
Traffic light bulbs, 13
Trains, 16-17
Travel, 11-24

Treasury Department, 36,
Treasury Postal Service, 69
Trenton, N.J. sewer, 62
Truck drivers, 12
Trucks, 12
Tyson Chickens, 67
Tzotzil, 83
U.S. Army Engineers, 63
U.S. Army School of the Americas, 52
U.S. Forest Service, 19, 34, 76
U.S. Naval Academy, 48
U.S. Postal Service, 68
Umbrellas, 56
Urban Mass Transit Administration, 23
Vacations, free, 82
van den Berghe, Pierre, 36
Vegetarianism, 86
Vice President's temporary residence, 39
Washington, University of, 36
Waste Isolation Pilot Plan, 89
Water, inhaling, 80
Wave-making machine, 8
Wilchusky, Le Ann, 19
Works Progress Administration, 64
Worms, constipated, 30
Xerox machine, 61
Yacht rental, 37
Zwynenburg, John, 70